CHINESE PROVERBS

ESSENCE OF ANCIENT WISDOM

CHINESE PROVERBS
ESSENCE OF ANCIENT WISDOM

4th Edition Published 2008
ISBN: 978-988-98269-6-3

©FormAsia Books Limited
706 Yu Yuet Lai Building
45 Wyndham Street
Central, Hong Kong

E-mail: formasia@formasiabooks.com
Website: www.formasiabooks.com

Introduction by Peter Moss
Chinese translations: Agnes Chen Wei-lan
Art Direction by Hans Lindberg
Digital Artwork by Kitty Chan
Calligraphy by Ian Leung
FormAsia Marketing Eliza Lee
FormAsia Archive Sathish Gobinath
Source of illustrations:
The Palace Museum – Beijing: Cover, 3, 12-13, 14-15,
17, 19, 20-21, 28, 33, 45, 52, 56, 60, 62, 64, 68,
70-71, 79, 81, 83, 87, 93, 95, 96-97, 98, 100, 102,
106, 108-109, 111, 113, 115, 117, 121, 122-123,
124, 130, 134-135, 139, 141, 142-143, 144, 148
Chang Dai-chien: 22, 24, 50, 54, 58, 71, 146
Qi Baishi: 47, 73, 75, 77
Hong Kong Museum of Art: 30-31, 35, 89
FormAsia Books: 26, 37, 39, 41, 43, 48-49, 66, 85,
91, 104, 119, 126, 128, 132, 137

Printed by RR Donnelly – China
Film separations by Sky Art Graphic Co., Limited

CHINESE
PROVERBS

ESSENCE OF ANCIENT WISDOM

FormAsia

CHINESE PROVERBS
ESSENCE OF ANCIENT WISDOM

Introduction

*I*t wasn't always Confucius who said it. Long before the aphorisms and analects of this venerated Chinese sage, born in 551 BC, began their ascent to international currency, establishing their author as a household name around the world, homilies and *mots juste* were being handed down through generations of his ancestors, both in writing and by word of mouth.

Once Sinophilia began to grip the west, in the wake of Marco Polo's account of his astonishing travels in that amazingly civilized region on the other side of the globe, it became fashionable to attribute almost any intelligent remark to Chinese sources. If Confucius hadn't actually said it himself, it must have come from one of his countrymen. Which was very often the case, except for the fact that many of them walked Chinese soil long before he did.

There is an aptness and eloquence to Chinese proverbs that, in every instance, makes the moral pungently recognisable and resoundingly true. Across the centuries, they impart a relevance that is timeless and universally applicable. Even after thousands of years we discover them to be so fresh and newly minted that we may ask ourselves "Why didn't I think of that?".

Their brevity encapsulates boundless dramatic possibilities, inviting conjecture as to their provenance. Who first advised that, when planning revenge, one should dig two graves? From what unhappy outcome of a long-festering vendetta was that lesson first learnt?

The majority of Chinese proverbs are eminently sensible and to the point. How indeed can you expect to find ivory in a dog's mouth? And what hope is there of extinguishing a fire in a cart-load of firewood with only a cup of water?

We may find, in these ancient distillations of wisdom, striking parallels with proverbs familiar to us from our own inheritance. In picking up a sesame seed, we can lose sight of a watermelon; a predicament akin to being penny wise but pound foolish.

And playing a harp before a cow is much the same as casting pearls before swine. Some prefer carrots and others cabbage is the vegetarian variant of one man's meat being another man's poison.

No wind without waves inevitably echoes no smoke without fire.
To pick up a stone only to drop it on one's own foot is of course the eastern equivalent of shooting oneself in that appendage. To mend the pen after the sheep are gone reminds us of a lock too late, bolting a barn door after the horse has been stolen.

Other Chinese bywords evoke poetry in their phrasing. To shed no tears before seeing the coffin is to be so stubborn as to persevere in an ill-advised course until it is too late.

Innocent of evil, we need not worry about devils at the door. So long as we bear in mind that the spear from in front is easier to dodge than the arrow from behind. And should we fail to take such lessons to heart, we should be conscious that, just as jade is worthless before polishing, so man is useless before education.

Then there are those adages less readily interpreted, painting word pictures in which we should look beyond first impressions. We can easily visualise one monk shouldering the water jar alone, two who share the labour and three who will go thirsty. But this is a scene that suggests far more than our version of 'two's company, three's a crowd.'

From the parable of the monks we are left to deduce that individual initiative can breed dependency, to the point where the more participants, the less achieved. So we end up reminded of a very different western equivalent, in this case of too many cooks spoiling the broth.

In other instances too, the sheer poetry of expression can be misleading, and not always what is first implied. The longer the night, the more we dream, far from being an encouragement to linger in that condition, is a wake-up call. It warns that the longer we stay in a disadvantageous position, the more risks we take.

Not a few proverbs are provocatively and gravely obtuse. To kill the chicken before the monkey is to set a cautionary example, by executing one in order to admonish a hundred, or warn the many by punishing the few.

Then there are those that are quite deliberately opaque, disguising their import in riddles whose very solution affords pleasure. To add legs to the snake after you have finished drawing it means doing something that is totally unnecessary and spoiling what you had already achieved.

To have one's ears pierced just before the wedding ceremony is an admonition of procrastination, conjuring an image of a bride suffering extreme discomfort on the wedding dais because she left that important particular to the last.

Of all animals in the Chinese bestiary, the tiger commands a special place. The Chinese say that man dies and leaves a name, whereas the tiger dies and leaves a skin.

They warn us not to escape the flood by clinging to a tiger's tail. But should we do so, happily for our posthumous condition, we can take comfort in the fact that a tiger never returns to an unfinished repast.

Which of us can forget that he who rides the tiger is afraid to dismount? Or that when the tiger dies, he does not lose his dignity? Nevertheless, the tiger descending to the plain is in danger of being insulted by dogs. Yet even so, another Chinese proverb cautions that if you miss the tiger, he won't miss you.

Even without tigers, the world can seem a dangerous place when there are always ears on the other side of the wall, when you're a flea seeking shelter on a bald head, when a weasel comes to say "Happy New Year" to the chickens, or when the undermining of an ant may well destroy a whole dam.

But consult the analects again and you will derive solace from the fact that a book contains a house of gold, that flies never visit an uncracked egg, that just as a son never deserts his mother for her homely appearance, so a dog won't forsake his master because of his poverty. And while good fortune may augur bad luck, so bad luck may in turn disguise good fortune.

Console yourself too that even a hare will bite when it is cornered, and accept that, of all the stratagems, knowing when to quit is the best. Then, with courage in your heart and conviction in your stride, you can embark on the proverbial journey of the thousand miles, resolved it must begin with the first step.

The wisdom gathered within these pages, then, is but the first step on a rewarding journey to the discovery of the far greater wisdom accumulated, over the millennia, by one of the oldest and greatest civilizations this earth has ever seen.

Peter Moss

COURT PAINTINGS OF
THE PALACE MUSEUM –
BEIJING

During the reigns of the brilliant Qing emperors Kangxi, Yongzhen and Qianlong, the court became a leading patron of the arts at a time of political stability and economic prosperity in their vast kingdom.

The Kangxi emperor, whose portrait appears on the cover of this book, consolidated the Qing state militarily and politically. He adapted his administration to the Confucian traditions of his predominantly Han subjects, over whom he ruled for more than 60 years. In addition, he was a master of Han Chinese culture, including calligraphy, as well as an intensely intelligent and curious interlocutor of Westerners who arrived in China and worked at his imperial court.

Kangxi's son Yinzhen, who became the Yongzheng Emperor in 1723, was renowned as a great administrator who implemented fiscal and administrative reforms. His short reign is famous for the production of exquisite decorative arts in the palace workshops.

The Qianlong Emperor, son of Yinzhen, in his turn assembled the largest art collection in history and was a prolific and highly talented poet, writing some 30,000 poems.

The arts of the Qing court were used by the Qing Emperors – themselves ethnically Manchu – to express and maintain their command of the diverse territories they ruled, from the Mongolian steppes and deserts of the north to the gardens and rice fields of the semi-tropical south.

Imperial China had little direct contact with the West during the reign of the three Qing emperors. However, these rulers were intrigued by Western technical expertise. A gallery within the Forbidden City housed paintings, clocks and decorative arts as evidence of Chinese interest in foreign expertise and innovation. These items, given as gifts to the emperors, illuminate the courtly relations with the Jesuits who travelled to China to seek converts to Christianity in the 16th and 17th centuries.

The most renowned Jesuit to be sent on a commission to the Imperial court was the artist Lang Shining, better known by his Western name of Giuseppe Castiglione (1688-1766). His paintings, intended primarily for the Western market, depicted nature in a detailed, literal manner and incorporated decorative Chinese characteristics. The fusion of Chinese and European modes was a key factor in defining the style of painting associated with the Qing court.

The Palace Museum was established on the site of the Imperial Palace in Beijing. The Palace, also known as the Forbidden City, was built in 1420. The properties of the museum comprise the former imperial collections of the Ming (1368-1644) and Qing (1644-1911) dynasties.

QI BAISHI (1864-1957)

Unlike the majority of China's greatest artists, Qi Baishi was born the son of a poor farmer. Born in 1864 in the province of Hunan, Qi's family was unable to afford his schooling, so he worked as a cowherd and carpenter before learning to paint at the age of 27. He started with folk pictures of gods, then moved on to painting landscapes, birds and human figures.

In 1918, after the collapse of the Qing dynasty, Qi Baishi moved permanently to Beijing. There his unaffected though graceful works did not find favour with connoisseurs, and Chen Shizeng, a fellow painter and fan of Qi Baishi's work, encouraged him to alter his meticulous style in favour of free sketching. With this inspiration, Qi Baishi began his programme of 'transformation' and virtually withdrew from society, placing on his door a sign that read, "Old man Baishi has had a recurrence of heart sickness and has stopped receiving guests."

After years of isolation and concentrated work, he achieved his unique style, which incorporated inspirational elements from his life. He dedicated his art in praise of nature at a time of social and cultural change in China. He retained his peasant philosophy and detested the manners of sophisticated city-dwellers, yearning instead for the leisurely life of the countryside.

Qi Baishi received the International Peace Award in 1955 and was named one of the Ten Cultural Giants of the World in 1962. He passed away on 16 September 1957.

Qi Baishi's paintings appear on pages 47, 73, 75 and 77.

CHANG DAI-CHIEN (1899-1983)

Chang Dai-chien was born 10 May 1899, in Nei-chiang, Sichuan, the ninth child of a wealthy family. Resisting a business career, he entered a Buddhist monastery before beginning intensive familiarisation with Chinese calligraphy and painting at the age of 19. Chang settled in Shanghai in 1919 to study with prominent artists. Employing a training method typical among art students in China, he made many copies of artistic masterworks, beginning to develop his legendary (and notorious) ability to recreate works from diverse periods.

The collapse of several family businesses in 1925 deprived him of his livelihood and compelled him to begin selling his artwork. His first exhibition of 100 paintings in Shanghai in 1926 was a great success and launched his career.

Leaving China in the wake of the Civil War of 1945 to 1949, Chang sojourned in Hong Kong, Taiwan, India and Argentina before settling in 1954 in Brazil. He travelled to Paris in 1956 for a breakthrough show of his paintings at the Musée d'Art Moderne. His encounter with Pablo Picasso during this trip was seen as a meeting of the masters of Western and Eastern art. Chang eventually relocated to Taiwan in 1976, spending his last years painting and creating his garden home known as the "Abode of Illusions."

In addition to his prized original works, Chang has become equally famous through his virtuoso talent for emulating, and even improving upon, the work of painters who preceded him. Today, many of these forgeries hang alongside Chang originals in museums worldwide.

Chang Dai-chien's paintings appear on pages 22, 24, 50, 54, 58, 71 and 146.

If you want happiness
for an hour, take a nap.
If you want happiness
for a day, go fishing.
If you want happiness
for a year, inherit a fortune.
If you want happiness
for a lifetime, help somebody.

BEAUTY

❖

The measure
of perfection

1

It is the beautiful bird
that invariably gets caged.

木秀於林　風必摧之

2

Light is good from
whatever lamp it shines.

有麝自然香

3

Everything has beauty,
but not everyone sees it.

造化之妙　知者能幾

4

Different flowers are
beautiful to different people.

各花入各眼

5

Avoid the employment of
servants too pleasing to the eye.

童僕勿用俊美

6

Dream different dreams
while in the same bed.

同床異夢

7

One man's fault is
another man's lesson

前車可鑑

8

Knowing is not as good as loving;
loving is not as good as enjoying.

知之不如好之 好之不如樂之

情殷鑑古

道光己酉清和月

Books

The transmitted
measures of
civilisation

1

Those who do not read are no
better off than those who cannot.

知而不行 是為不能

2

Study without reflection is a waste of time;
reflection without study is dangerous.

學而不思則罔 思而不學則殆

3

If you wish to know the mind of
a man, listen carefully to his words.

言為心聲

4

After three days without reading,
talk becomes flavourless.

三日不讀 便覺語言無味 面目可憎

Learning is a treasure that will follow
its owner like a shadow everywhere.

學為寶庫　永遠傍身

A vacant mind is open
to all suggestions as a hollow
building echoes all sounds.

胸無城府　人云亦云

The beginning of wisdom is
to call things by their right names.

名正則言順

Real knowledge is to know
the extent of one's ignorance.

自知無知　為知者也

9

Life is finite, while knowledge
is infinite.

生也有涯 而知也無涯

10

A book is like a garden
carried in a pocket.

書中自有黃金屋

11

A closed mind is like a closed book;
no more than a block of wood.

思想不開放 封閉像塊木

12

Learning a lesson never ends.

學無止境

27

拾

13

There are no mistakes, only lessons.

經一事 長一智

拾

14

Good advice, like good medicine,
is difficult to swallow.

良藥苦口利於病 忠言逆耳利於行

拾

15

When we lose, we don't lose the lesson.

行而有失 不失教訓

拾

16

Who is not satisfied with himself will
grow; who is not sure of his own
correctness will learn many things.

滿招損 謙受益

FAMILY

❖

Man's heritage
and only hope
of succession

1

If the family lives in
harmony, all affairs will prosper.

家和萬事興

2

To understand your parents' love,
raise children yourself.

養子方知父母恩

3

Life is partly what we make it, and
partly by the friends whom we choose.

生命憑自主 擇友能輔之

4

Once you are poor, neighbours
close by will be distant; once rich, you'll be
surprised by visits from relatives afar.

窮在路邊無人問 富在深山有遠親

5

Every day cannot be a feast of lanterns.
花無百日紅

6

A dog won't forsake his master
because of his poverty; a son never deserts
his mother for her homely appearance.
兒不嫌母醜 狗不嫌家貧

7

If a son is uneducated, his father is to blame.
子不教 父之過

8

When eating bamboo sprouts,
remember the man who planted them.
飲水思源

9

A room common to
many will be swept by none.

三個和尚沒水吃

10

Easier to rule a
kingdom than to run a family.

國易治而家難齊

11

When you go outside, watch the weather;
when you come inside, observe people's faces.

在外看天色 屋內看臉色

12

Deal with the faults of
others as gently as with your own.

恕己及人

拾

13

With true friends... even water
drunk together is sweet enough.

知心能相聚 喝水也心甜

拾

14

When brothers and sisters argue
the bystander takes advantage.

鷸蚌相爭 漁人得利

拾

15

Giving your son a skill is better than
giving him one thousand pieces of gold.

遺子黃金滿簏 不如一經

拾

16

Hire a young carpenter
but consult an old physician.

量才而用

17

Love your neighbours, but
don't demolish the fence between.

防人之心不可無

18

Vegetables of one's own raising are not as
relished as those from another's garden.

本地薑不辣

19

One's good deeds are only known
at home; one's lesser deeds far away.

好事不出門 壞事傳千里

20

A friend is the one who enters in
when the whole world has departed.

患難見真情

貳拾壹
21

Never do anything standing that
you can do sitting, or anything sitting
that you can do lying down.

殺雞焉用牛刀

貳拾貳
22

Have a mouth as sharp as a
dagger but a heart as soft as tofu.

刀子嘴 豆腐心

貳拾叁
23

At birth we bring nothing with us
at death we take nothing away.

生不帶來 死不帶走

貳拾肆
24

Man who waits for a roast duck to fly into
his mouth must wait a very, very long time.

守株待兔

貳拾
25

Even the most clever housewife
does not cook without rice.
巧婦難為無米炊

貳拾
26

Much talk does not cook rice.
空談不能飽肚

貳拾
27

There is no never-ending
banquet under the sun.
天下無不散之筵席

貳拾
28

Fool me once, shame on you;
fool me twice, shame on me.
愚我一次貽爾羞　愚我者再我則恥

貳拾 29

Not wine but men intoxicate themselves;
Not vice but men entice themselves.

酒不醉人人自醉

叁拾 30

If you see in your wine the
reflection of a person not in your
range of vision, stop drinking.

適可而止

叁拾 31

After praising the wine,
they sell us vinegar.

掛羊頭 賣狗肉

叁拾 32

You can't expect both ends
of a sugar cane to be sweet.

針無兩頭利

Fauna

The commonality
of all living
organisms

1

Black cat or white cat:
If it can catch mice, it's a good cat.
不管黑貓白貓　能捉老鼠是好貓

2

Experience is a comb which
nature gives to men when they are bald.
人老賺經驗　只是難回頭

3

Crows everywhere are equally black.
天下烏鴉一樣黑

4

When you have only two pennies
left in the world, buy a loaf of bread
with one, and a lily with the other.
靈糧與食糧　兩者不可缺

5

Give a man a fish and he will
eat for a day. Teach a man to fish and
he will eat for the rest of his life.

釣勝於魚

6

Govern a family as you would
steam a small fish – very gently.

治大國若烹小鮮

7

Go home and make a net if you
desire to catch fish.

臨淵羨魚 不如退而結網

8

With time and patience the
mulberry leaf becomes a silk gown.

只要有恒心 鐵杵磨成針

9

Trees may prefer calm,
but the wind will not subside.
樹欲靜而風不息

10

The best time to plant a tree
was twenty years ago.
The second best time is today.
亡羊補牢 未為晚也

11

To cultivate trees, you need 10 years.
To cultivate people, you need 100 years.
十年樹木 百年樹人

12

Even the mighty
oak was once an acorn.
英雄莫問出處

拾

13

A smart rabbit will have
three entrances to its den.

狡兔三窟

拾

14

Even a hare will bite when cornered.

趕狗入窮巷

拾

15

Don't build a new ship out of old wood.

朽木不可雕也

拾

16

It is only when the cold season
comes that we know the pine and
cypress to be evergreens.

歲寒然後知松柏之後凋也

拾 17

A bird in your hand is worth
more than 100 in the forest.
一鳥在手 勝如百鳥在林

拾 18

If I keep a green bough in my
heart, the singing bird will come.
心中有枝葉 引得黃鶯留

拾 19

You cannot prevent the birds of
sorrow from flying over your head,
but you can prevent them from
building nests in your hair.
哀愁雖飛過 莫任府中留

貳拾 20

An ant may well destroy a whole dam.
千里之堤 潰於蟻穴

貳拾

21

Judge not the horse by his saddle.

人不可以貌相

貳拾

22

Distance tests the strength of horses;
only time reveals the hearts of men.

路遙知馬力 日久見人心

貳拾

23

You think you lost your horse?
Who knows, it may someday return
with a stable of horses.

塞翁失馬 焉知非福

貳拾

24

Once a word leaves your mouth, you cannot
chase it back even with the swiftest horse.

一言既出 駟馬難追

貳拾 25

When your horse is on the brink of a
precipice, it is too late to pull in the reins.

懸崖勒馬收韁慢 船到江心補漏遲

貳拾 26

A dog in a kennel barks at his fleas;
a dog hunting does not notice them.

大人不檢細行

貳拾 27

You can't expect to find ivory
in a dog's mouth.

狗嘴裏吐不出象牙來

貳拾 28

The lean dog shames the master.

狗瘦主人羞

29

Extraordinary like a crane standing
amidst a flock of chickens.

鶴立雞群

30

Even a horse may stumble on four feet.

人有失手　馬有失蹄

31

Add legs to the snake after
you have finished drawing it.

畫蛇添足

32

Nothing ventured, nothing gained.

不入虎穴　焉得虎子

He who rides a tiger is afraid to dismount.

騎虎難下

With money you are a dragon;
without – a worm.

有錢一條龍　無錢一條蟲

Going to law is like losing
a cow for the sake of a cat.

拾了芝麻　丟了西瓜

Donkey's lips don't fit onto a horse's mouth.

驢唇不搭馬嘴

叁拾柒 37

A swallow cannot know
the lofty ambition of an eagle.

燕雀安知鴻鵠之志

叁拾捌 38

When you paint a dragon,
forget not to dot its eyes.

畫龍須點睛

叁拾玖 39

When you paint a dragon you paint his
scales, not his bones; when you see a man
you see his face, not his heart.

畫虎畫皮難畫骨 知人知面不知心

肆拾 40

Do not kill the hen for the eggs.

莫殺雞取卵

自稱臣是酒中仙

丙子夏月

散輝廿三兄屬寫君家太白行吟狀喜家上元岳人筆法圓秘堂氣中發

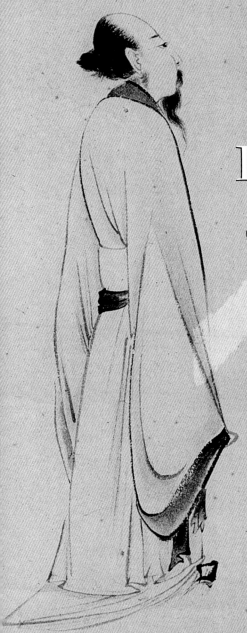

KNOWLEDGE

The harvest reaped
from the seeded
soil of learning

1

If you know, to recognize that you
know. If you don't know, to realize that
you don't know: That is knowledge.

知之為知之 不知為不知 是知也

2

What you do not wish upon
yourself, extend not to others.

己所不欲 勿施於人

3

True knowledge is when one knows
the limitations of one's own knowledge.

人貴有自知之明

4

Do not want others to know what you
have done? Better not have done it anyway.

若要人不知 除非己莫為

A clear conscience fears not
that midnight knock.

平生不做虧心事 半夜敲門也不驚

He who denies all — confesses all.

此地無銀三百両

If you want happiness for an hour,
take a nap. If you want happiness for a day,
go fishing. If you want happiness for a year,
inherit a fortune. If you want happiness
for a lifetime, help somebody.

小睡怡神片刻 垂釣輕鬆一日

遺贈享樂一年 助人幸福一生

Never hesitate to ask a lesser person.

不恥下問

9

If you want to know your past —
look into your present conditions.
If you want to know your future —
look into your present actions.

想知前世事 今生受者是
想知來世事 今生作者是

10

Diseases can be cured; fate is incurable.

病可醫 命運難移

11

When the ear will not listen,
the heart escapes sorrow.

耳不聽 心不煩

12

Choose a job you love, and you will
never have to work a day in your life.

樂業則無苦工

拾

13

A fall into a ditch makes you wiser.

喫一塹 長一智

拾

14

I was angered, for I had no shoes. Then I
stumbled across a man who had no legs.

知足常樂

拾

15

Sour, sweet, bitter, pungent,
all must be tasted in the journey of life.

嘗盡酸甜苦辣

拾

16

A gem cannot be polished without
friction, nor a man perfected without trials.

玉不琢不成器 人不學不知理

17

A man without a smiling face
must not open a shop.
不能笑臉迎賓 切莫開店待人

18

To open a shop is easy, to
keep it open is the art of survival.
創業容易守業難

19

One person tells a falsehood and a
hundred repeat it as being the truth.
謠言說百遍便成真理

20

There are always ears
on the other side of the wall.
隔牆有耳

貳拾 21

If you are patient in one moment of anger,
you will escape a hundred days of sorrow.

忍得一時之氣 免得百日之憂

貳拾 22

Seeing it once is better
than being told one hundred times.

百聞不如一見

貳拾 23

To guess is cheap.
To guess wrong is expensive.

猜揣方便 猜錯價高

貳拾 24

Take a second look...
it costs you nothing.

小心無大過

貳拾

25

Great fortunes depend on luck;
small fortunes depend on diligence.

大富由天　小富由儉

貳拾

26

Make no promises when you are seized by joy;
write no letters when you are seized by anger.

喜時多失言　怒時多失理

貳拾

27

To be truly happy and contented, you must
let go of what it means to be happy or content.

知足常樂　源自無求

貳拾

28

A murder may be forgiven,
an affront is never forgiven.

士可殺　不可辱

貳拾 **29**

Tell me and I'll forget; show me and I may
remember; involve me and I'll understand.

言語易忘 眼見能記 參與能通

叁拾 **30**

Failure is the foundation of success
and the means by which it is achieved.

失敗乃成功之母

叁拾 **31**

Learning that does not
daily increase will daily decrease.

學不日益則日損

叁拾 **32**

If you neglect your art for one day
it will neglect you for two.

拳不離手 曲不離口

33

If you must play, decide on three
things at the start: the rules of the game,
the stakes, and the time to quit.

玩遊戲，先決者三：規則、注碼及離場時間

34

Do no favours purely for their rewards.

施恩莫望報

35

Make happy those who are near,
and those who are far will come.

近者說　遠者來

36

The tongue is like a sharp knife,
it can kill without drawing blood.

舌劍殺人不見血

叁拾柒

37

He who could foresee affairs
three days in advance would be rich
for thousands of years.

能知三日事 富貴幾千年

叁拾捌

38

Those who say it cannot be done
should not interrupt those doing it.

己所不能 勿阻人為之

叁拾玖

39

A single fact is worth a
shipload of arguments.

事實勝於雄辯

肆拾

40

The best place to find a helping
hand is at the end of your own arm.

求人不如求己

41

A smile will gain you ten more years of life.

笑一笑 十年少

42

They who know the truth are not equal to
those who love it, and they who love it are
not equal to those who find pleasure in it.

知之者不如好之者 好之者不如樂之者

43

An inch of time is worth an inch
of gold, but you cannot buy that inch
of time with an inch of gold.

一寸光陰一寸金 寸金難買寸光陰

44

A word whispered in the
ear can be heard for miles.

耳邊私語 可傳萬家

When you bow, bow low.

既來之 則安之

He who sacrifices his conscience for
ambition burns a picture to obtain the ashes.

為野心而毀良知 如焚丹青求灰燼

To talk goodness is not good.
But to do so is.

口惠不如實至

A man who has committed
a mistake and doesn't correct it
is committing another mistake.

過而不改 是謂過矣

MOUNTAINS

The monuments
to nature's
achievement

There are many paths to
the top of the mountain, but
the view remains the same.
一致而百慮 殊途而同歸

Even the highest
mountain begins at the base.
萬丈高樓平地起

Climb mountains to see lowlands.
登高望遠

The man who removes a mountain
begins by carrying away small stones.
高山可以移 需從片石始

5

Men trip not on mountains –
they trip on molehills.

小河溝裏翻船

6

No matter how strong the wind howls,
the mountain will never bow to it.

大山不為狂風折腰

7

Enough shovels of earth – a mountain.
Enough pails of water – a river.

積土成山 積流成河

8

I dreamed a thousand new paths... In the
morning I woke and walked my old path.

夢裏千般 醒來依舊

9

Only the man who crosses the river at
night knows the value of the light of day.
事非經過不知難

10

Only he that has travelled the road
knows where the holes are deep.
事非經過不知難

11

To know the road ahead,
ask those coming back.
要知前頭路 須問過來人

12

Do not look where you fell,
instead where you slipped.
勿念其失 必求其因

拾

13

If you walk on snow you
cannot hide your footprints.

人過留跡 雁過留聲

拾

14

A journey of a thousand
miles begins with a single step.

千里之行 始於足下

拾

15

Better to be deprived of food
for three days, than of tea for one.

寧可食無肉 不可居無竹

拾

16

Coarse rice, water and a bent
arm for a pillow — happiness may be
enjoyed even in these.

飯蔬食 飲水 曲肱而枕之 樂亦在其中矣

拾

17

Wherever you go,
go with all your heart.

悉力以赴

拾

18

Blind men hear what deaf men see.

盲者聽 聾者視

拾

19

When a finger points at the moon,
the imbecile looks at the finger.

一犬吠影 百犬吠聲

貳

20

Better late than never,
but better never late.

遲到好過不到 最好還是早到

OF GREAT MEN

The models
of lesser men's
ambitions

A single conversation with a wise man
is better than ten years of study.
與君一席話 勝讀十年書

Great souls have wills;
feeble ones have only wishes.
大人有志 小人有願

He who asks a question is a fool
for five minutes; he who does not ask a
question remains a fool forever.
不知則問 其惑一時
不知而不問 惑其一生

Great thoughts come from the heart.
智由心生

5

There is a great man who makes every
man feel small. But the really great man is
he who makes every man feel great.
有些偉人令人自覺渺小　真正偉人令人自覺重要

6

Age and time do not wait for anyone.
歲月不饒人

7

Be not afraid of growing slowly,
be afraid only of standing still.
不怕慢　只怕站

8

We are not so much concerned if you
are slow as when you come to a halt.
不怕慢　只怕站

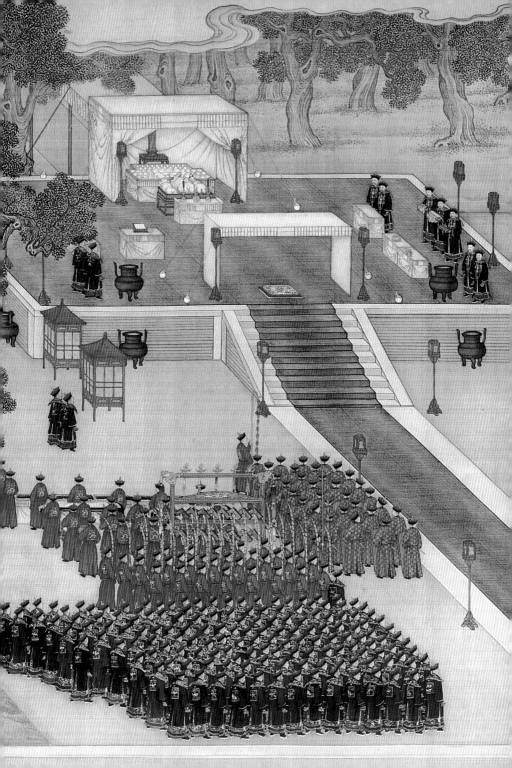

9

Preserve the old,
and yet acknowledge the new.

溫故而知新

10

Laws control the lesser man.
Right conduct controls the greater one.

小人靠法治　君子賴德行

11

Behind every able man,
there are always other able men.

山外有山　人外有人

12

The saving man
becomes the free man.

儉故能廣

拾
13

A wise man makes his own decisions,
an ignorant man obeys public opinion.
智者靠己 庸者靠人

拾
14

Small men think they are small;
great men never know they are great.
渺小的人認為自己渺小
偉大的人從不知道自己偉大

拾 佐
15

If a man does only what is required
of him, he is a slave.
If a man does more than is required
of him, he becomes a free man.
塞責者為奴 負責者為主

拾
16

It takes little effort to
watch a man carry a load.
隔岸觀火易

拾
17

A man must insult himself
before others will.
人必自侮而後人侮之

拾
18

Better to argue with a wise man
than to prattle with a fool.
寧與智者辯 莫與愚者聊

拾 玖
19

It is not the knowing
that is difficult, but the doing.
知易行難

20

Teachers open the door,
but you must enter by yourself.

師父領進門　修行在個人

21

Simplicity of character is the most
natural result of profound thought.

深思熟慮　則反樸歸真

22

Be kind to unkind people;
they need it the most.

仁以待不仁　裨益其所缺

23

A great man can bend and stretch.

大丈夫能屈能伸

WAR

The fires that
forge courage
and endurance

1

He who cannot agree with
his enemies is controlled by them.

善與敵謀 方能制人

2

Of all the thirty-six alternatives,
running away is best.

三十六着 走為上着

3

Take not a musket to kill a butterfly.

殺雞焉用牛刀

4

A day of sorrow is
longer than a month of joy.

悲傷難過 歡樂易忘

If there is light in the soul,
there will be beauty in the person.
If there is beauty in the person,
there will be harmony in the house.
If there is harmony in the house,
there will be order in the nation.
If there is order in the nation,
there will be peace in the world.

心正而後身修
身修而後家齊
家齊而後國治
國治而後天下平

The greatest victory is the battle not fought.
不戰而屈人之兵 善之善者也

The best soldiers are not warriors.
人不可以貌相

8

The more you sweat in peacetime,
the less you bleed during war.

平時多流汗 戰時少流血

9

The rise and fall of a nation
rests with every one of its citizens.

國家興亡 匹夫有責

10

Better an open enemy than a false friend.

明槍易擋 暗箭難防

11

Thousands of bones will become ashes
before a General achieves his fame.

一將功成萬骨枯

Forget insults, never forget kindnesses.

有仇不念 有恩勿忘

The soldier who retreats 50 paces jeers at the one who retreats 100.

五十步笑百步

Attack is the best defence.

進攻是最佳的防守

He who seeks revenge should remember to dig two graves.

冤冤相報只會同歸於盡

拾陸
16

Those who play the
game do not see it as clearly
as those who watch.

當局者迷 旁觀者清

拾柒
17

An enemy will agree,
but a friend will argue.

忠言逆耳

拾捌
18

A hundred men may make
an encampment, but it takes a
woman to make a home.

安營需百夫 持家需一婦

WATER

The fount of
life and source
of tears

1

Dismantle the bridge
but only after crossing it.

過河拆橋

2

Once you pour the water out of
the bucket it's hard to pour it back.

覆水難收

3

Distant water won't
quench your immediate thirst.

遠水解不了近渴

4

No wind, no waves.

無風不起浪

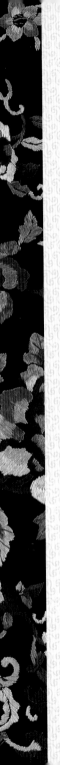

One man will carry two buckets of
water for his own use, two men will
carry one for their joint use; three men
will carry none for anybody's use.

一個和尚挑水吃
兩個和尚擔水吃
三個和尚沒水吃

The wise adapt themselves to
circumstances, as water moulds
itself to the pitcher.

人之隨時猶水之隨器

When you want to test the
depths of a stream, don't use both feet.

人前只説三分話 未可全交一片心

The water that bears the ship
is also the water that engulfs it.

水能載舟　亦能覆舟

When drinking water, remember the source.

飲水思源

A bird can roost but on one branch, a mouse
can drink not more than its fill from a river.

弱水三千　只取一瓢飲

When the blind lead the blind,
they will both fall into the water.

盲人騎瞎馬　夜半臨深池

WORSHIP

The tribute of the gods

1

Respect the gods and respect the
devils – but keep them at a distance.

敬鬼神而遠之

2

Better do a good deed near to home
than go far away to burn incense.

千里燒香不如隨處行善

3

Better to light a candle than
to curse the darkness.

臨淵羨魚 不如退而結網

4

To the ruler the people are heaven;
to the people food is heaven.

君以民為本 民以食為天

5

People with virtue must speak out;
people who speak out are not all virtuous.

有德者必有言　有言者未必有德

6

He who depends on himself
will attain the greatest happiness.

自求多福

7

Blessings do not come in pairs;
misfortunes never come singly.

福無雙至　禍不單行

8

It is not necessary to
light a candle to the sun.

多此一舉